W9-CLW-001

NOT A BUZZ to Be FOUND

Insects in Winter

LINDA GLASER   illustrations by JAIME ZOLLARS

MILLBROOK PRESS · MINNEAPOLIS

Thanks to Jennifer Sazama,
fellow nature lover and
children's book enthusiast
—LG

For Griffin, who loves
finding bugs in his garden
—JZ

The publisher wishes to thank scientific consultant Larry Weber, retired teacher, author, and naturalist

Text copyright © 2012 by Linda Glaser
Illustrations copyright © 2012 by Jaime Zollars

Millbrook Press
A division of Lerner Publishing Group, Inc.
241 First Avenue North
Minneapolis, MN 55401 U.S.A.

Website address: www.lernerbooks.com

Main body text set in Tapioca ITC Std 20/28. Typeface provided by International Typeface Corp.

Library of Congress Cataloging-in-Publication Data

Glaser, Linda.
    Not a buzz to be found : insects in winter / By Linda Glaser ;
Illustrations by Jaime Zollars.
        p.   cm.
    ISBN 978–0–7613–5644–8 (lib. bdg. : alk. paper)
    1. Insects—Hibernation—Juvenile literature. 2. Insects—
Wintering—Juvenile literature. 3. Insects—Behavior—
Juvenile literature. I. Zollars, Jaime. II. Title.
    QL467.2.G56 2012
    595.7—dc221   2011001148

Manufactured in the United States of America
1 – PP – 7/15/11

In summer, insects are all around
zipping, buzzing, zooming everywhere.
But in winter, *poof,* they're all gone!
Not a zip or a buzz or a zoom anywhere.

Where do insects go when it's icy and cold?
What do they do to survive?
If you were a little insect,
what would you do to stay alive?

If you were a monarch butterfly,
you'd take an amazing flight!
You'd fly thousands of miles,
migrating south where it doesn't freeze.

There you'd join millions of monarchs all gathered together in trees.

What if you were a woolly bear caterpillar?
You'd hide under a blanket of snow or leaves.
Someday you'd turn into a moth with wings.

But in winter, you'd curl up and sleep, sleep, sleep.

If you were a ladybird beetle,
you'd hide under logs or leaves
and huddle with thousands of others.

8

You'd barely move or breathe.

What if you were a honeybee?
You'd eat the sweet honey in your hive
and huddle with all the other bees.
You'd all stay warm together,
each taking turns in the warmest spot—the center.

10

If you were a
mourning cloak butterfly,
you'd hide under the bark of a tree
and go into a deep, deep sleep.
But you wouldn't freeze. Why not?
You'd have something inside you like antifreeze.

What if you were a praying mantis?
You'd still be an egg in a small egg case
with hundreds of others waiting to hatch.
All winter long you'd stay snug and safe.

If you were a Common Pondhawk dragonfly,
you'd still be a baby nymph without wings.
You'd look like a small water bug
and live in a pond way down in the mud.

16

If you were an ant in winter,
you'd stay underground in your nest
with the other ants in your colony.
Safe from the cold, you'd all just rest.

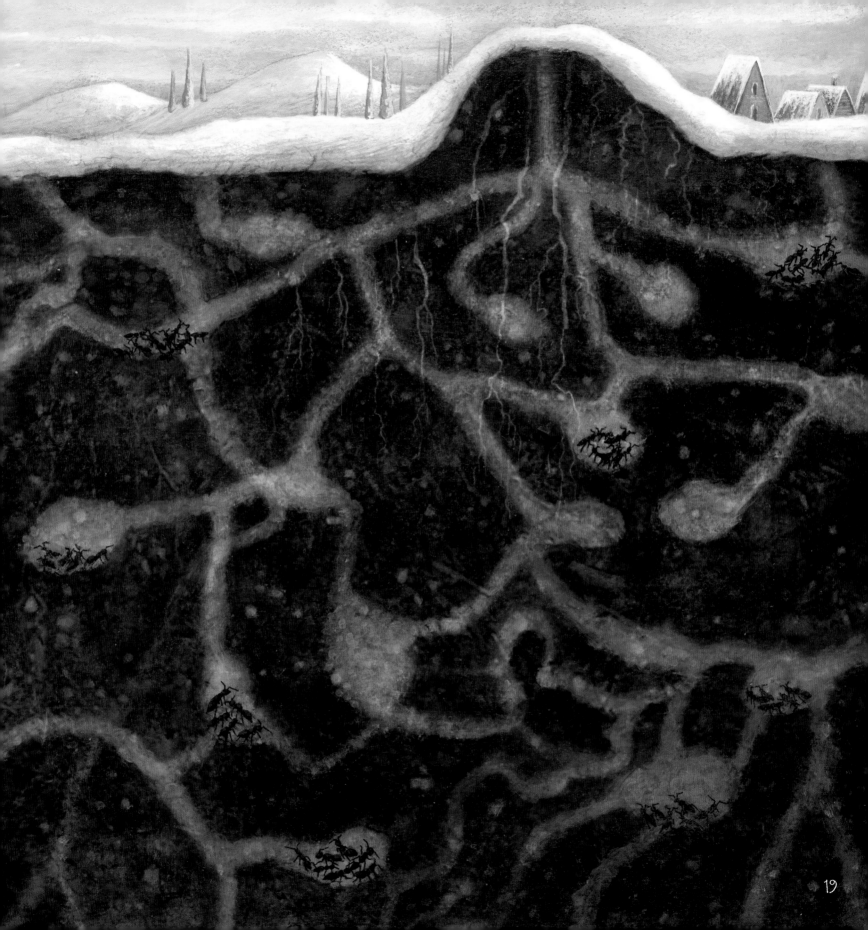

19

If you were a **gallfly** in winter,
you'd still be a baby living in a gall.
You'd chew a little opening to get out in the spring.
But all winter you'd stay in that small round ball.

20

What if you were a field cricket?
You'd still be a tiny egg that mother cricket laid.
All winter long you'd stay in the earth.
Safely hidden, you'd wait and wait.

If you were a bald-faced hornet queen,
you'd crawl into a rotting log and hide.
You'd stay fast asleep all winter
with your baby eggs safe inside you.

If you were a black swallowtail butterfly,
you'd still be a caterpillar
without any wings.

Inside your chrysalis,
safely hidden,
you'd sleep all winter,
just waiting for spring.

26

Then slowly, slowly the air grows warmer.
And just as slowly the days grow longer.
You feel a change in the air
and so do insects everywhere.

Some wake up. Some hatch.
Some fly north. Some grow wings.

It's time to zip and buzz and fly.
Winter is over. At last, it's spring!

MORE ABOUT THE INSECTS

Monarch Butterfly

The monarch is the only tropical butterfly that lives part of its life far from its warm home. It migrates to places all over the United States and southern Canada. The only monarchs that migrate back to warm climates are the ones born in the fall. They fly thousands of miles to spend winter in either California or Mexico. None of these monarchs have ever migrated before. Yet, somehow, they find their way to the very same wintering spots that their great-grandparents found the year before!

Woolly Bear Caterpillar (Isabella Tiger Moth)

The woolly bear caterpillar sleeps all winter. When an insect takes a long sleep during any part of its life cycle, it's called diapause. The woolly bear caterpillar makes a substance called glycerol that works like the antifreeze in a car. This keeps the caterpillar from freezing. (Many insects make this antifreeze in their bodies in winter.) In spring, the woolly bear caterpillar wakes up and spins a cocoon. In a week or two, an Isabella tiger moth comes out of the cocoon.

Ladybird Beetle (Ladybug)

As babies, ladybugs look sort of like tiny alligators. They turn into full-grown ladybugs before winter. In winter, they usually gather in large groups and huddle together to stay warm. In spring, they scatter, flying off in many directions.

Honeybee

Before winter, all the drones (the males) are pushed out of the hive. There would not be enough food for all of them. Only the queen bee and the other females spend winter in the hive. They huddle together to stay warm. They eat the honey that the worker bees collected during the warmer months.

IN THIS BOOK

Mourning Cloak Butterfly

The mourning cloak butterfly spends winter as an adult butterfly. It hides under the bark of a tree or under dead logs. The mourning cloaks also produce a substance that works like antifreeze. So they don't freeze even when the temperature drops.

Praying Mantis

In fall, the mother praying mantis produces a foamy froth on a plant. She lays about two hundred eggs in it. This froth hardens and becomes an egg case. This case is so hard the eggs are protected for winter. In spring, they hatch. Out come tiny praying mantises without wings. The babies eat and grow. They shed their skin a few times and finally become fully grown adults with wings.

Common Pondhawk Dragonfly

Common Pondhawk dragonflies are commonly found in the eastern United States. The adult females are green, and the adult males are mostly blue. The nymphs (babies) stay underwater down in the mud all winter. When spring comes, they crawl out of the water onto a plant stem. They shed their skin and emerge as adults with wings. Some other insects that do this are mayflies and stone flies.

Ant

Most ants eat more than usual during the fall. This gives them extra fat to live on during the winter. When it gets cold, some ants huddle beneath the tree bark. Other ants crawl into the walls of houses. Many gather in colonies deep in their underground nests. The opening to their nest becomes closed off with soil or sand that collects over it. The only type of ant that eats during winter is the harvester ant. These ants take seeds into their nests to eat during the cold months.

Gallfly

The female gallfly sticks her sharp, pointy back end into the stems of goldenrod plants. She lays her eggs in them. When the larvae (babies) hatch, they eat the inside of the stem. Their saliva causes the plant to grow a gall. This is a round ball on the plant stem. Each larva lives in its own gall on its own stem. In fall, the larva cuts a small opening in the gall. As winter comes, the gallfly larva creates an antifreeze substance in its body so it doesn't freeze. In spring, the baby gallfly turns into an adult gallfly with wings. It leaves the round gall through the small opening it made in fall.

Field Cricket

In fall, the female cricket pokes her back end into the ground and lays her eggs. The eggs stay underground all winter. In springtime, baby crickets hatch. They look like tiny adults, but they don't yet have their wings. The babies shed their skins as many as ten times. The final time, they emerge with wings. The males are the ones that "sing" by rubbing their wings together.

Bald-Faced Hornet

The queen is the only bald-faced hornet to survive the winter. She carries eggs inside her. She spends winter in a rotting log or under the bark of a tree. In spring, she starts building a new paperlike nest. She then lays her eggs in it. Soon the eggs hatch, and a new colony of hornets has begun.

Black Swallowtail Butterfly

In fall, the swallowtail caterpillar spins a long silk thread. It uses the thread to attach itself to a twig. Then it wraps itself with the thread and creates a chrysalis. The chrysalis turns green or brown to match its twig. It blends in and looks like part of the twig or branch. That way, it stays well hidden. In spring, the swallowtail butterfly emerges.